STRAND PRICE
$ 5.00

D0679895

I DON'T NEED A BABY
TO BE WHO I AM

Also by Joan Brady

God on a Harley
Heaven in High Gear

Published by POCKET BOOKS

I DON'T NEED A BABY TO BE WHO I AM

Thoughts and affirmations on a fulfilling life

Joan Brady

POCKET BOOKS

New York London Toronto Sydney Tokyo Singapore

POCKET BOOKS, a division of Simon & Schuster Inc.
1230 Avenue of the Americas, New York, NY 10020

Copyright © 1998 by Joan Brady

All rights reserved, including the right to reproduce
this book or portions thereof in any form whatsoever.
For information address Pocket Books, 1230 Avenue
of the Americas, New York, NY 10020

ISBN: 0-671-00980-X

First Pocket Books hardcover printing March 1998

10   9   8   7   6   5   4   3   2   1

POCKET and colophon are registered trademarks of
Simon & Schuster Inc.

Printed in the U.S.A.

This book is dedicated with hugs and kisses to my precious Katie, Kevin, Brian, Tara, Jimmy, Kristen, Tommy, Emily, Megan, Peter, Chrissy, Jake, Jack, and Patrick.

ACKNOWLEDGMENTS

A very special thanks to Denise Stinson and to Emily Bestler, whose foresight, sensitivity, and literary expertise resulted in this, our third project together. I am also grateful to the brave women in history who cleared a path through traditional thinking and who began making it possible for women to celebrate our choices, our individual paths, and our lives.

CONTENTS

CONTENTS

PREFACE

This is a book for women who have not walked the traditional, well-beaten path to the delivery room. It is for women who, for whatever reasons, have not become mothers.

Many writers will tell you that writing a book is a lot like having a baby. From the first hints of new life, right down to choosing a name for the finished product, this book has certainly been no exception. I felt "pregnant" with the idea for several months before I went into "labor" and sat down to actually "deliver" it.

The idea for this book came to me unexpectedly, much the way pregnancy often occurs. At first, I tried to ignore the nagging symptoms that a book with a life of its own wanted very much to be written. In addition to the effort I knew this would require, I also had to come to terms with the fact that there might be some discomfort, inconvenience, and even great pain involved, but in the end, I knew, like any mother, it would all be worth it.

Someone once told me that an unfinished manuscript is like a fetus, beautiful only to its mother until it is completely formed, delivered, and cleaned up.

I showed this manuscript to many people, long before it was mature enough to survive on its own. Even when it was nothing more than an idea to write something, anything, about women who have never given birth and to explore my own feelings about being one of them, the enthusiasm I encountered was enormous.

Everyone had a friend, a relative, or a colleague, it seemed, who would appreciate a book like this. Apparently there are many women who feel they are forgotten, overlooked, cheated, and shunned by society because they have not fulfilled the traditional role of motherhood.

I understand that each and every one of us who is childless has a unique story to tell, whether we are struggling with infertility, the loss of a child, or, like me, simply have never found acceptable circumstances in which to have a child. I can only write from my own experience, and that is what I have done in these pages. I don't pretend to truly understand the depth of anyone's pain but my own, and I freely admit that I am no expert on anything but myself. But that is all it took to turn my pain into joy. Becoming an expert on myself.

This is only my story, and I do not imagine that it can encompass the magnitude and the depth of all the similar stories that are out there. I only hope that some of the skills and insights I have found may also be successfully applied to other problems and to other people.

My purpose for writing this book was to let other women like me know that they are not alone. They are not the only ones who feel different or left out or inadequate, and knowing that you are not alone can be the first step toward healing.

My hope is that if you are in pain, you will find something in these pages that will make you feel that at least one other person has been there too and that there is something positive waiting for you. My message is one of hope that we can all evolve to our highest level of being, and that we will all learn to think well of ourselves.

There were times while I was writing, particularly in the first section about the painful years, when it was just too agonizing to go back and dig up all of those old, torturous memories. At those moments when I found myself unable to write another word, simply because I didn't want to relive the torment of those years, I was tempted to trash the whole project. But something in me knew that this was too important a subject to retreat from because of a transient thing like pain. Like most of us, I've had lots of discomfort in my life, and like a mother in labor, I supposed I could give that one last exhausting push in order to initiate a new life.

With the help of some very smart friends, I found ways to trick myself into bearing the pain of those old memories. I resorted to writing the most uncomfortable memories in the third person, as though I were writing about someone else who had gone through this, and somehow that made it much easier to put the true essence of my story onto the paper. I suppose I was afraid that if I looked too closely at those painful years, there might be a very real chance of crippling myself again.

My path toward wellness and a strong sense of identity and purpose was not traveled easily, and it was not without setbacks. The road toward enlightenment was not a straight course, but rather filled with unexpected twists and turns, and I sometimes followed that path only one baby step at a time. Oftentimes, I feared that I might not make it, that there were just too many obstacles and no one to show me which way to go. But finally, one day I looked back and was astounded to see the length of the road behind me.

What I came to realize, however, was that in the course of evolving beyond my limited thinking about motherhood, I also learned how to resolve a lot of other issues that had always had a way of cropping up in my life. Most of the skills I've developed, I now apply effectively to various other areas of my life, the most important skill being stepping back and seeing the big picture.

Thankfully, it is now almost impossible for me to imagine that there was once a time when I saw my life as a giant vacuum, when I was convinced that joy was something only other people experienced. I don't even recognize that person who used to think she couldn't be happy unless everything turned out the way she thought it should.

The greatest joy I have found has come from letting go of all my expectations and experiencing my life one glorious moment at a time, the way a mother experiences her child. I have learned that my life is far more fulfilling when I take it as it comes, giving it everything I've got and expecting nothing in return but the unfolding of a deep mystery.

I am about to take you on a journey. We set sail from the painful, frightened years and emerge into the calm beauty of awakening. Finally, we will cruise gracefully into a celebration of the female joy that has been kept secret for so long. This journey is not for the faint of heart. Travelers are required to be courageous, honest, and mature. It is a process born of great pain, but the rewards are enormous, and the new life that emerges is something to behold.

At last, I have learned to be both the mother and the child in my own life, and each role contributes something of great value. The mother in me keeps me strong and nurtured, and the child keeps me resilient and open to possibility. The combined energy of these two puts a smile in my heart.

And it's about time.

PART ONE

The Painful Years

CHAPTER ONE

The Spinster Nightmare

It wasn't the bogeyman, monsters under the bed, or even getting a shot at the doctor's office that terrified me most as a child. My biggest fear was that I might grow up to be like my poor aunt Agnes, the one who never married and who never had children.

Aunt Agnes was living proof that there are no guarantees in life and that was what frightened me so. It seemed that all little girls were expected to grow up, get married, and have families; so, to my six-year-old way of thinking, Aunt Agnes was a deviation from all that was normal. She was the only woman I knew who never had a husband or a baby, and that seemed to separate her from all the so-called "normal" people in the world.

No one ever spoke openly about her life circumstances, and I learned at an early age that questions regarding the matter were strictly off-limits. The world seemed to pity Agnes, and there was always an air of tragedy and emptiness about her. From a very young age, I was certain I didn't want my life to turn out like hers.

I was positive—because everyone had told me so—that I was going to grow up to marry a wonderful man and have lots of babies with him. Marriage and motherhood were presented to me as the ultimate goal, and I spent many joyful childhood hours preparing for those roles. My best friend and I "played house," vowed to be bridesmaids at each other's weddings, and dreamed of our wedding day as we pushed our toy baby strollers around the block.

Yet, even in the midst of such blissful daydreaming, I do remember some disturbing doubts creeping in about just how joyous a life that might actually be.

Take "Betsy Wetsy," for instance. She was a very popular baby doll when I was growing up in the 1950s. She came complete with a plastic baby bottle that could be filled with water, a hole in her mouth that fit perfectly over the nipple, and a cloth diaper that became wet a moment after she was "fed." While other little girls marveled at this doll's lifelike qualities, it occurred to me what a chore she really was. Being one of seven children myself, I had already fed and diapered my share of real babies. At the tender age of eight, I was beginning to ask questions more appropriate of twenty. What was so fun about this? Why did I need another hungry mouth to feed or another dirty diaper to change? What I found most disturbing of all was that no one seemed to have much of an answer for me, other than this was supposed to be a young girl's idea of entertainment.

Though I wanted to believe that life would be perfect once I found a husband and had a baby, the circumstances that I saw around me didn't always validate that belief. There were times when I delighted in cuddling and playing with my infant siblings, but there were also times when motherhood looked suspiciously like a never-ending chain of chores. Nagging doubts began creeping in, and I began feeling torn between the desire to be a mother and the wish to have a life that included adventure, freedom, and independence. I even wondered if God had made a mistake when he made me and had really intended me to be a boy. Quite honestly, building tree forts looked like a lot more fun than changing Betsy Wetsy's soaked diapers, but, of course, statements like that were frowned upon.

My biggest concern was that if I didn't hold tight to the motherhood dream, I would be cast into a world that would probably eat me alive. Who would protect me? Who would love or care about me? What possible purpose could I serve? Even more frightening, Who would show me the way if my way wasn't motherhood? What else were girls supposed to do? I had no idea. I knew there were women who never married or had children, but it seemed the best they could hope for was mere survival. You never heard of them flourishing or being ecstatically happy. No, spinsterhood was too scary a prospect. Forcing myself to fit in seemed like the only logical answer.

In the end then, I decided to swallow my nagging doubts. After all, my options appeared quite limited. During the 1950s, even if a little girl had her eye on a career, the only ones open to her seemed to be nursing or teaching.

Since I was never very fond of school, I certainly didn't think I wanted to spend my adult life in a classroom, so I chose nursing as my profession. Besides, everyone told me it was only until I got married, right? I guess that somehow explained the notoriously low salaries of nurses and teachers.

I listened carefully to the messages that my Irish, Catholic, conservative world was giving me, and I did all the things I thought were expected of me. I finished high school, graduated college, and most important, kept my eye open for Mr. Right.

Only Mr. Right never showed up. Or maybe I just didn't notice him. By my late twenties, I decided that he must have been killed in Vietnam, since so many of my virile young peers had been sent there. For a time, I even thought that probably the federal government should send me some kind of monetary compensation for having killed my husband, even though I hadn't met him. How could I have if they had drafted him to some remote corner of the world, then asked him to die for his country?

Whatever the reason, Mr. Right hadn't shown up, and he was screwing up my plans. How was I supposed to get married and have all those children that were expected of me if he never showed his face?

In my early twenties, I had begun going to a lot of other people's weddings, and I remember overhearing relatives ask my parents, "Joan isn't married yet, is she?" As another decade marched by, I remember hearing the same question, only now it had a slightly more urgent tone to it, "Joan still isn't married, is she?" Later, when I reached forty and had not wed, the question sounded altogether different, "Joan never married, did she?" The first time I heard it put that way, I felt as if someone had kicked me in the stomach. In other words, it was far too late for a normal life.

Somewhat dejectedly, as my twenties rolled on, I watched my sisters, brothers, cousins, and friends marry and start their families, and all I could think was, What is wrong with me? Why can't I find someone to settle down with? To have a baby with? To make my life feel normal?

The relationships I was drawn to at that time in my life were not healthy ones. It seemed the only romantic alliances that attracted me were dramatic, turbulent, and often my affection went unrequited. As desperately as I thought I wanted the commitment of marriage and family, on some level I knew it would be unfair to subject, not myself only, but an innocent baby as well to the

emotional roller coaster of the unstable and imma-
ture relationships to which I was so consistently
drawn.

Of course, there was always the option of just
having a baby anyway, without the added compli-
cation of marriage, but I had to honestly ask myself
what my motivation for this was. The answer was
not pretty. Put simply, I was just plain lonely. And
maybe a little bored as well. Neither was a good
enough reason to have a baby, as far as I could see.
In spite of having been socialized to believe that
motherhood would fill me with an enormous
sense of satisfaction and that raising children was
the ultimate feminine fulfillment, I also began to
wonder why, if this were so, were so many foster
homes filled to overflowing? As usual, I found
people evaded answering my question.

Whenever I mentioned it to others, I consistently received the same answer, "You'll feel empty
and lonely later in life if you never have children."
That didn't really scare me because I was feeling
empty and lonely anyway. The next question that
kept creeping into my mind was, Why are the
people who are telling me this, all people who are
married with children? How can they possibly
know about something they have never experi-

9

enced, and why am I listening to them? In fact, Is there anyone else out there who's in my position? It sure didn't feel as though I had many peers, but then, among the people I knew, no one really talked much about women like me. It wasn't polite.

I decided that I had too much reverence and respect for children to use them as a remedy for my own sense of emptiness and loneliness. I would get a pet if the loneliness ever became that unbearable. By my late twenties, I realized I didn't even want *that* much responsibility, since there were plenty of things I still wanted to do, like travel and write and run a marathon. If I wasn't even ready for a pet in my life, what made me think I was ready for a child? Besides, I still had time.

I decided to take my chances and put my life in the hands of fate. I would just accept life the way it happened to me, and there would be no more trying to force a square peg into a round hole. No more trying to be like everyone else, just for the sake of fitting in. I decided to be very brave and trust in the order of the universe and in myself, trust that whatever was meant to be would be. I realized that the route to motherhood, though filled with its own perils, was a well-traveled one with lots of company and signposts along the way. The offbeat direction that I was headed in was largely unknown to me and, for all I knew, might very well lead to the same place, but I was prepared to take my chances.

I didn't know it then, but I was heading toward the land of women who never marry or have children, and mercifully perhaps, I had no idea what lay ahead.

As I tiptoed into my early thirties, I tried to remain calm while I stripped my psyche of all those traditional expectations. I traveled and advanced in my career as a nurse. I published a few articles and even ran a marathon. Not surprisingly, those industrious years flew by in a blur of activity, and suddenly I was thirty-five, a milestone that I'd heard made you officially middle-aged. Now, more and more often, the unmistakable yearnings for a child returned. Was it because I longed for the happiness and fulfillment a child is supposed to bring? Or was I just afraid of losing my options? I honestly didn't know. But the longings were so strong at times, they were actually a physical ache in my arms, my belly, and my heart. There were moments when I was so filled with maternal love I thought I might explode if I didn't have someone upon which to bestow it.

By my late thirties, the prospect of finding a suitable marriage partner looked pretty grim, but all of my earlier ambivalence about motherhood suddenly was gone. I desperately yearned for a child now. I knew I had an enormous amount of love, devotion, and talent to share with a daughter or a son, and I considered my childlessness a great injustice and a terrible tragedy. Why was it so difficult to find a partner to share the fulfillment of these longings? Where was that other half of me that everyone promised would show up in my life?

I still wasn't willing to have child without a capable and devoted mate. Not that it couldn't be done alone, I supposed, but I wanted to give my child every advantage. I felt I had a responsibility to provide my offspring with a stable home life, one that included two parents—one to caretake and one to provide. I was willing to play either role, but not both. Like the female of almost every species, I carefully watched for an appropriate mate and father for my unborn children. When Mr. Wonderful didn't show up, I did my best to ignore or squelch those aching maternal urges. I tried to bury them under a career and to numb them with food and sometimes with alcohol, but always they bubbled to the surface of my consciousness and demanded my attention.

Panic set in as forty loomed near, and I began thinking a lot about my poor spinster aunt Agnes. How did she know when she had had her last date? Had she had any clue the last time someone kissed her good-night on a date that that was it for the rest of her life? Had I had my last date and I just didn't know it yet?

When I saw people who had been divorced or widowed and who had then remarried and started their "second" families, I felt very cheated indeed. I hadn't even found one eligible partner, while so many people had found two or more. The hardest part of all, though, was when friends and acquaintances commented that they had always assumed I simply didn't want to have children or else, certainly, someone as stubborn and independent as me would have had them. Even more painful, they sometimes assumed that I simply didn't like children.

They had no idea.

When my dreaded fortieth birthday became a reality, I found myself magnetized by those talk shows where couples struggling with infertility told their tearful stories. I suppose I felt they were the closest thing I had to peers, since they were the only people I knew who appeared to be hurting as much as I was. I truly understood the longing and the frustration they were feeling, and I ached for them. I was like a giant sponge that absorbed other people's tears in those days, then wrung out some of my own in the process. I listened to teenage girls, on the same talk shows, who insisted on becoming mothers while they were still in high school. Because of my own acute loneliness, I realized that often these girls wanted so desperately to be loved by someone that they had decided to create that someone, a baby, to love them. The idea was not foreign to me, and though I couldn't condone voluntary teenage pregnancy, I fully empathized with them.

By this time, bridal showers had become uncomfortable at best, and baby showers had become pure torture. No one but another woman who longs for a child can even begin to grasp the degree of heartache I felt at these outwardly joyous events. I continued to attend all of them, out of a sense of obligation to be gracious, but all the while I was consumed with what felt like my own very personal brand of pain.

I watched my nieces and nephews and the children of my friends growing up, and that, too, had become almost unbearable. Everything seemed to be a reminder that time was marching on relentlessly and that there was no returning to my sugarcoated girlhood dream of motherhood. It wasn't until I noticed that no one ever asked about my own plans for marriage and family anymore that I realized my worst nightmare had come true.

I had become my aunt Agnes.

CHAPTER TWO

The Mothers' Club

The path that led me out of those years of confusion, ambivalence, and longing did not follow a straight line. Frequently it seemed I would take two steps forward then one step back. Some insights occurred to me in my twenties and others in my thirties, only to be forgotten or brushed aside until they showed up again more clearly in my forties.

Somewhere around my mid twenties, I began to notice the emergence among my friends of an exclusive sorority I came to call the Mothers' Club. It involved a nine-month "hazing period," followed by a particularly painful "Hell Night," after which one was granted a lifetime membership in a group

that is highly revered and respected by most socie-
ties.

The members of the Mothers' Club that I knew
were women who once were just like me and with
whom I'd once had so much in common. We had
shared things like lengthy, late-night phone calls,
leisurely lunches in outdoor cafés, and supporting
each other as we maneuvered our way up the
career ladder. Our lives seemed to be in synchro-
ny. We knew each other's politics, philosophies,
dreams, and goals. We could laugh at the silliest
things and not have to explain. At times, it seemed,
we could almost read each other's minds. We
never seemed to run out of things to talk about,
and we were secure in the knowledge that we were
always on the exact same wavelength.

Until they got pregnant.

After the first of my good friends became pregnant, I noticed that everything changed. Calendars
suddenly became crucial. What had once been
used to plan vacations or seminars was now a
necessary tool in calculating the exact date of
conception and the expected date of delivery. I
stood back and watched as the entire focus of my
friend's life shifted to unfamiliar concepts like
trimesters, sonograms, and lunar months as op-

posed to calendar months. Conversations now centered around vitamins, fetal development, and the emotional impact of a name.

At first I thought that this particular girlfriend was a little obsessed and that everything would return to normal after the baby was born. I couldn't have been more wrong.

One by one, I watched every one of my pregnant friends go through the same process. This was a very odd and confusing time for me. After having spent their prepregnancy days bemoaning minor figure flaws, they were now actually grateful if they had wide hips. For the first time in their lives, most were suddenly very happy with their breast size, and a protruding little belly was now an object of great pride.

As each one began her journey through pregnancy and into motherhood, I learned to quietly look elsewhere for companionship. Despite their initial protests that our friendship wouldn't change because of this new experience, I already knew that our lives would be like two speeding trains going in opposite directions. Sadly, I realized that unless (by some miracle) I suddenly joined the Mothers' Club too, things between us

could never be the same again. The entire com-
plexion of our relationship was bound to change.

Pregnancy was only the first leg of my friends'
journey. The most profound changes occurred
once they had actually given birth and then became absorbed in the daily routine of caring for
their babies, which inevitably caused us to drift
even farther apart. Motherhood apparently
spawned a whole new outlook on life for them,
along with a completely different set of priorities. I
witnessed each of my friends go through some
kind of mystical transformation, right before my
eyes, wherein they became thoroughly engrossed
in the magnitude of creation, leaving me to wonder what it was like to be so thoroughly passionate
about and committed to something that hadn't
even existed this time last year. It wasn't that these
women weren't interested in my life anymore, but
their own blossoming new roles had simply become almost all-consuming for them.

It was as though everything that had preceded
motherhood was somehow sloughed off and left
behind. Our old friendship was now replaced by
burgeoning bonds with other new mothers. The
hardest part for me to accept was the almost

foreign way in which they all related to each other. There was something special, almost reverent about it, and I was not a part of it.

I began to feel like an alien in what had once been familiar and comfortable territory. Suddenly, my old cronies developed strange new powers of intuition, like sensing that their baby was crying, even though they were ten miles away at work. They developed odd little rituals, like calling home every chance they got, and tried to be in bed by nine P.M. if at all possible. Gone was the possibility of late-night phone calls, Saturday afternoon nail appointments, and even shared chocolate bars at work. Now that most were breast-feeding, they were more devoted to health and nutrition than they had ever been when it was just for their own good. I missed the old days.

They even spoke a new and unfamiliar dialect in which age was measured in months rather than years. It took an embarrassingly long time for me to figure out that a twenty-two-month-old was not the same as a two-year-old. Go figure.

Another newly developed talent of members of the Mothers' Club was the uncanny ability to recognize each other instantly, whether at work, in the supermarket, or in the locker room at the gym.

Formal introductions apparently were not necessary in order to *ooohhhh* and *aaahhhh* over the latest pictures of each other's children. And they focused on details in those pictures that totally escaped the likes of me. Women who once had nothing in common now gladly swapped delivery-room horror stories and offered each other heartfelt support and understanding of each other's fatigue. They acted like people who had known each other all of their lives and were quick to trade cute little anecdotes that only another mother could truly appreciate. Little by little, I began to feel terribly left out.

Not that I didn't know what it was like to love a little baby. I totally understood how easy it was to just lose yourself in the allure and the charm of those cuddly, soft little bundles. I had felt those same powerful emotions for the first time at the age of six, when my little brother was born. He was the most fascinating thing I'd ever seen, and I lavished him with all kinds of "big sister" love. Even at that young age, I remember having an overwhelming urge to love and protect and teach him. I would sit by his bassinet for hours at a time, just watching him do extraordinary things like breathe and yawn and smile. I was no stranger to

2 1

the joy of nurturing a baby, and it is clear to me now that those powerful maternal instincts were with me even then.

But since my brother, I had had no one on whom to bestow that kind of attention and love. There were times when I wanted desperately to be included in that whole miracle of procreation, moments when I physically ached to hold a baby of my own, but I still held on to a thin thread of hope that my soul mate would appear, and so I waited. Though I was truly happy for the women who did immerse themselves in the joy of motherhood, it gradually became painful for me to witness it.

By the time I was thirty, the Mothers' Club had become very popular among those I knew, and the vast majority of my friends and acquaintances had joined it. At first, I had merely felt confused by the metamorphosis I had witnessed in so many of my friends, but now I was beginning to feel like the unathletic child who never gets picked for the team. I began asking anyone who would listen, "What is wrong with me?" "Why hasn't my life started yet?" "What if it never happens to me?" Rather insidiously, I went through a metamorphosis of my own, and it wasn't a pretty sight.

Although I had a career that challenged and

stimulated me, I felt something important was missing from my life. Parks and playgrounds became dangerous places for me. I would find myself fighting back tears every time I saw a little boy reach for his mommy's hand or a little girl swing her hair in that incredibly feminine gesture that they seem to acquire naturally. I began to resent being invited to other people's baby showers, and I did whatever I could to avoid showing up. Shopping for gifts had to be done, but I resented that too. Baby clothes no longer touched a tender chord of hope in my heart, but, rather, reminded me of all that I did not have.

I was no longer awed by pregnancy, nor did I experience the old sense of enthusiasm for the miracle of childbirth, especially after so many of the women I knew began having their second and third babies. Now I often found myself becoming annoyed with the self-absorbed and exuberant behavior of new mothers. I had about as much patience for their maternal zeal as I had for the enthusiasm of people who tried to convert me to a new religion.

I became quick to criticize and even faster to point out the inequities I had to suffer as a result of other people's having babies. Eventually I began a downward spiral into despair and jealousy as I focused on all the negative ways in which I thought the Mothers' Club was imposing on my life.

For instance, why did it seem that I was always expected to work holidays so that members of the Mothers' Club could spend that special time with their children? Why wasn't my time considered special anymore? I didn't want to hear about Christmas traditions that families shared. I had my traditions too. They were the ones that only non-Christians and single people like me discover on those miserable, family-oriented holidays. We are the small minority of American society who know the only places open for business on Christmas are movie theaters and Chinese restaurants. Those were my traditions.

And what was the big deal about traditions anyway? I wondered. As far as I could see, it was just a way of concentrating on our differences instead of on the things that we can all share. I had no shortage of loving and generous invitations on those special occasions, but the fact is, it was just too painful to show up alone. It was far easier to get bitter and to remove myself from the festivities. Resentment felt a whole lot better than the utter loneliness and hopelessness of those painful days.

Now I knew how the dinosaurs must have felt when the world evolved around them, eventually reducing them to mere fossilized remains.

Bitterness metastasized throughout my heart, and what had once been my deepest desire had now hardened into something rather ugly and selfish. I questioned why I should have to pay taxes for school systems and playgrounds that I would never use. I became irritated when friends I called would insist on putting their toddler on the phone, for what they considered a very entertaining few minutes of baby garble.

I also noticed that most women become hard-of-hearing upon becoming mothers. How else could they be so oblivious to the high-pitched whines and endless chatter of their two-year-olds? And don't get me started on teenage mothers and welfare. Why was I being punished because some teenager had made an irresponsible choice? I had gone out of my way to make responsible choices in my life and to postpone having children until I knew I could provide for them. This whole situation seemed terribly unfair to me.

If I'd had the time, I could have come up with enough resentment to fill an ocean. I was angry, disappointed, and defensive. It seemed that everywhere I went in those painful years, I would see pregnant women patting their bellies. I was easily annoyed by crying babies in department stores, and I often walked out of restaurants if I saw even one young child who had the potential to become cranky.

Little by little, I turned my attention elsewhere and simply refused to think about it. I had successfully blocked others from prying into my childless state, so now the only reactions I had to control were my own, and that was fairly easy. That is, until the day my best friend gave me an unexpected glimpse of motherhood, and my heart began breaking all over again.

It was the middle of August, and my friend came to visit me in the late afternoon with her newborn daughter. We sat on the couch, chatting and laughing, while she rhythmically rocked her baby. I remember noticing that everything seemed bathed in white at that moment—the couch, the chiffon curtains billowing in the late summer breeze, even the baby's blanket and the T-shirts we all wore.

The baby fussed, and my friend casually lifted her T-shirt and began breast-feeding, without missing a beat of our conversation. Gradually, though, our words trailed off as we both became engrossed in the sound of the baby's contented suckling.

It was an incredibly beautiful and feminine moment, one I will never forget. For some reason, the mystery, magic, and power of feminine energy was immensely apparent in the stillness of that room, and I automatically equated it with the undeniable beauty of motherhood.

In that moment, my bitter defensiveness had melted away, and I was once again filled with an aching desire to have a baby.

CHAPTER THREE

Hitting Bottom

I always wondered how you knew when you had hit rock bottom. Naively, I thought I'd hit it the first time I realized that I had become what other people casually refer to as a "spinster." That was just the beginning. As miserable as I felt about my single status, I sank to an even deeper level of despair after several years of feeling shut out of the Mothers' Club. The fear that I could always descend to an even more intense level of misery than the one I was currently in lurked just below the surface of my every waking thought.

How low could I possibly sink? I wondered. It frightened me to think that there was no limit to just how unhappy I could become. If nothing else,

I wanted some kind of assurance that my situation at least would not get any worse. In my many years as a nurse, I had seen patients use the same kind of logic to "bargain" with pain. They had often told me that they could endure a dressing change or a wound debridement as long as they knew that after that, the wound would get better. Now I understood.

Of course, I knew I was focusing only on what I did not have, as opposed to what I did have, but that thought did not soothe me. I was feeling like a failure, a leftover, and about as useful as a broken clock. I wanted what everybody else seemed so effortlessly to have, and I felt as if I had been overlooked. More important, I just didn't want to hurt anymore. I thought that there should be some kind of flashing red light signaling the end of that downhill road, letting you know when you finally hit the bottom of despair. At least then you could take heart in the fact that it wouldn't get any worse.

Metaphorically, I did get a flashing red light, though at first I didn't recognize it for what it was. I was working at the hospital one evening, preparing the charts of seven patients who were scheduled for surgery the next morning. As I scurried from room to room, checking on blood work, urine specimens, and surgical consents, I couldn't help but overhear the conversation of some visitors standing outside of one young patient's room.

"It's such a tragedy," I heard one of them say. "She's so young." They spoke in hushed, sympathy-drenched whispers in the hospital corridor, lest the heartbroken, pathetic figure in the bed hear them.

The patient was only twenty-six years old and about to undergo a hysterectomy in the morning, thus ending any possibility of having "children of her own." Her hospital room had been transformed into a virtual botanical garden of exotic plants and flowers sent by well-meaning, supportive friends. A crowd of visitors surrounded the patient's bed like sentries at their post, watching, guarding, and protecting her from an adversary that was far bigger than all of them—a society that is not necessarily supportive of women without children.

As the registered nurse in charge of her care, I observed the scene while I maneuvered my way through the packed room. There was the distraught husband holding his wife's hand, the best friend lovingly wiping away the occasional stray tear that slipped down the patient's cheek, and the concerned relatives who stood outside the door, nervously drinking coffee and valiantly holding back tears of their own.

I was forty-one years old at the time, and in more than twenty years as a nurse, I had seen my share of tragedies, catastrophes, and plain old misfortunes. Professionally speaking, there was nothing new or shocking to me anymore, yet I found myself consumed with an emotion that I had never once experienced in all those years of hospital dramas.

God forgive me, I was jealous.

I am ashamed to admit it, but I had sunk to a new low that night and envied the frightened-looking woman in the hospital bed. Even though the deluge of sympathy she was receiving wouldn't last forever, she at least got to be a tragic figure, if only for a fleeting moment. The world was aware of her pain, and she was surrounded by people who were willing, not only to acknowledge her grief, but also to share their strength and love with her. They sent flowers, kissed her cheek, and prayed for her.

My loss, however, was not so visible. My reproductive years had simply slipped away one day at a time, quietly and without fanfare. I couldn't bear to think about the loss of this option after a while, because it was just too painful. It was clear by now, though, that I was heading down a path vastly different from that of most of the women I had encountered in my life.

I was forced to learn what every pioneer knows and what my young preoperative patient was about to learn—carving out a new role for oneself is never easy.

It wasn't sympathy or tolerance that I was looking for, it was acceptance, with perhaps a little respect sprinkled in, and it wasn't forthcoming. Women who never become mothers, for whatever reason, are frequently assigned several different labels, and none of them are pretty: "barren," "sterile," "childless," . . . "alone." My conservative, Catholic background had conditioned me to think that if I didn't give birth to a genetic look-alike, my life didn't count for very much. The messages bombarded me from every direction that I am incomplete, inadequate, and less than feminine if a baby never gestates in my womb. No one ever told me what to do if my life took a turn down a different path.

Now, for the sake of my young patient, her well-intentioned relatives were suddenly trying to discredit those age-old messages, but the lessons were too deeply ingrained and she had been taught far too well to take their words seriously. There were lots of forced smiles and light chatter that night about adoption and foster children, but my patient wasn't buying any of it. I looked at her lying in the hospital bed, as the fact of the impending surgery hung over her like the mushroom cloud over Hiroshima, and I knew that, as with the bomb, no one had to tell her what it meant.

After tomorrow, her body and her expectations would be permanently altered, and no matter how well-adjusted she became, from now on, baby showers and other people's children would remind her that she was "different." She would have to carve out a new identity for herself along with the rest of us who, for one reason or another, march to the beat of that different drum. In all likelihood, she would, at least for a time, come to resent that damned different drum beating where a fetal heart should have been. The misery on her face said it all, and it set off a familiar ache in my own heart.

Because I had seen it so many times, I felt I knew the rest of her story only too well. Once she recovered from the surgery itself and her survival was no longer in doubt, the sympathy and support would gradually fade away. She would probably go through a period of mourning and feeling cheated, but she might find that after a very short while most people would not be so eager to talk about it. She would soon learn that she had to walk that path alone, and she would have to find an inner core of strength to heal the wound in her heart.

So that was the night, though no flashing red lights or railroad gates had come down to warn me, that I realized I was in a very unhealthy state of mind. I somehow stood outside myself and recognized that envying my patient for the sympathy and acknowledgment she was receiving was as low as I was willing to sink.

Why had I allowed other people's opinions to be more important than my own? I had swallowed the traditional expectations of women without question and adopted them as mine. I had accepted other people's definition of failure and had willingly crawled into a corner of society long ago set aside for women like me who don't conform. In a moment of incredible clarity, I realized I had willingly contributed to the nightmare I was living.

I had lived in dread of being a spinster, only to become one. I had feared the emptiness of life without children, only to watch my childbearing years slip away unused. I had allowed others' expectations and myths surrounding marriage and motherhood to push me into a corner, where I lay loathing myself, licking my wounds, and crying from the pain of an emptiness so vast I thought nothing could fill it. I had believed that these "unfeminine" circumstances would make me miserable, and so they had.

How could I have been so blind? I, a registered nurse who had spent significant time watching the removal of female reproductive organs in the operating room! How could I not have noticed that a surgeon's scalpel doesn't remove our femininity? The essence of womanhood was obviously not rooted in our wombs or ovaries! I'd witnessed this surgery many times, and never had I seen a pathology report come back listing a woman's femininity among the excised specimens that were sent to be studied under the microscope.

I looked at my patient again, and I thought of the many others like her whose plans of motherhood had been halted. I thought about the pain and the bitterness that had followed. I thought of all the tears and heartache, including my own, that I had witnessed through the years. I had erroneously concluded that Nature was a traitor and played the cruelest of jokes on her own kind—women.

After all, I had reasoned, Nature has equipped our wondrous female bodies with the awesome ability to carry and sustain new life. She endows us with an almost limitless capacity to love and nurture a child. She blesses us with maternal instincts that are so keen we know exactly what a small child needs long before he or she is even capable of asking for it.

Nature lays all of these gifts at our feet and then doesn't allow some of us to use them. Why, I had wondered, would she give us this enormous power only to snatch it away in the guise of disease, circumstance, or some not-yet-understood reproductive malfunction? And Nature was capable of changing her mind too. She could plant the seeds of a new life in a woman's womb and in her heart, then suddenly decide that no, never mind, this baby wasn't meant to be.

I had taken all of this very personally and had become as resentful as any of my patients. I needed to be angry with someone, and Nature or Fate or whatever you want to call it made as good a target as any.

Until that night in the hospital, I had been too caught up in my own anguish and self-pity to realize that motherhood is only one part of the essence of womanhood. I hadn't been able to see the big picture because I had been staring too hard at a little corner of it. As with one of those pictures whose image emerges only when you stand back from it and relax, until I stopped concentrating so hard on the loss of one option, all I could see was pain and frustration.

If I had been able to let go of my pain and my struggle to fit in, I would have seen the obvious. I would have recognized the immense capacity that all women have to create, to love, to teach, to nurture, and to heal. I would have realized that the feminine embrace is not limited to any one function. We have been blessed with the mighty ability to love all life forms in a way that knows no bounds, and no genetic codes.

Standing in the hospital corridor that night, I finally understood that a woman's talents and instincts are unalterable. These gifts can never be rendered useless, and they endure in spite of outdated labels and attitudes, or even the surgeon's scalpel.

I'm still not sure what opened my eyes, but

somehow the first little seed of awareness had managed to sprout amid my disillusionment. Up until that night, my adult life had felt like a bad dream. With this first realization of the vast, perennial nature of my femininity, I felt I could almost touch the bountiful life that awaited me.

All I had to do was wake up.

PART TWO

The Awakening

CHAPTER FOUR

Fitting In

Opening my eyes to the world of childless women was a lot like waking up in the very early morning, not necessarily unpleasant, but confusing and a bit unwelcome. At first I felt disoriented in this environment that I had resisted for so long, yet I was awed at the idea of what might lie before me to be discovered.

Once I had stopped protesting and began to examine my new surroundings, I was surprised that they seemed ripe with possibility. No longer focused on what I didn't have, I sensed great potential all around me, and I had an abundance of time and energy to spend on whatever talents and issues piqued my interest. That was the good

4 1

news. The bad news was that though I certainly wasn't alone on this path, there seemed to be a stigma attached to being part of this group. It seemed to me that no matter what I might achieve, I would also be known for what I had not achieved: motherhood.

I began to notice how often other people just assume all women are mothers. I became annoyed when it seemed even casual acquaintances thought it natural to ask how many children I had. Worse than the assumption of motherhood was the awkward silence that followed when I said I didn't have children. Friends and acquaintances didn't seem comfortable talking about women like me, and they often awkwardly changed the subject. But finally, in spite of the social awkwardness, I was beginning to awaken to a sense of genuine excitement about all the other options that were available to me.

Though I was curious to see what treasures this different path might reveal, I also felt compelled to give voice one more time to over forty years of conditioning. Lying awake at night, I struggled with such questions as, What could possibly be the fate of a woman who doesn't bear children? Who would love me when I'm old? Who would inherit my worldly goods? Who would be motivated to keep my memory alive once I was gone? Though I knew there are no guarantees on those issues, even for those who have children, the questions still disturbed me.

If I didn't ask the questions though, how was I ever supposed to find the answers? The new possibilities? Other ways of living? How was I supposed to find the road that would lead to my own unique brand of happiness? Or was I to assume, like many of the people in my life, that childless women can never be completely happy? After all, I was taught from an early age that one source of true happiness comes from a sense of belonging, and that is something that outcasts, simply by definition, cannot possibly have. Or could I? It was time to find out.

There is probably no better feeling in the world than knowing that we are right where we belong and that we are among like-minded people. Though it's subtler in nature, for me that sense of belonging ranks right up there with essentials like a satisfying meal, heat in the winter, and a good night's sleep.

Usually, we get our first taste of belonging as children, when we are surrounded by our nuclear family. Our world is small at that time, and so our opinions and thoughts are limited to the small handful of people to whom we are exposed. We automatically "fit in," and we don't doubt our attitudes, our abilities, or ourselves. At least, that's how it all felt to me as a child.

Standing on the cusp of menopause, I found myself awakening to where I'd been for some time, to a lifestyle that, though it could be exciting, veered off the beaten path of the vast majority. I was a woman who would very likely not have children. I felt uneasy as I looked around and pondered my fate, feeling like a wounded animal that had been left behind by the herd. My once solid sense of belonging had dwindled as I watched everyone else move on with their lives. Here in hushed solitude, I could quietly obsess on the question of how I would be remembered, if I were remembered at all.

My question was answered unexpectedly the day a two-alarm fire broke out in the apartment complex where I lived.

I awoke at five A.M. on a Saturday morning, wondering what had disturbed me and why I couldn't get back to sleep. I felt restless and uneasy, like one of those animals who senses danger moments before it occurs. Someone then buzzed me on the intercom, and I shot out of bed, heart pounding, wondering who would be buzzing me at that hour. I picked up the intercom and hoarsely whispered "Yes?" into the phone.

"There's a fire next door!" a panic-stricken voice announced to me and several other sleepy tenants who'd answered their intercoms at the same time. "You better get out of the building!"

With that, I reached for clothing, shoes, and a sweater. I remembered to feel the door for heat before daring to open it, then ran out to the main lobby and through the front door as black smoke billowed from the building next door and orange sparks floated down from the inferno that raged above me. I had nothing with me but the clothes on my back, not even my purse, but suddenly I remembered the diamond ring that had been passed down through generations of women in my family and had once belonged to my spinster aunt Agnes, and I actually considered racing back inside to get it.

Of course my better judgment told me not to do anything so foolish, but why did that ring suddenly seem so important to me? Was it because the heart of my existence was somehow connected to it? Was it because it was tangible evidence of from where and whom I came? And if so, to whom would I leave that ring, and who would ever feel connected to me?

As I stood outside, mesmerized by the flames and shivering more from this brush with danger than from the cold, a revelation began to take shape in the back of my mind. I had recognized a familiar look on the shocked and confused faces of the residents as they made their way out of the burning building. Where had I seen that look before? It had an almost childlike quality to it, like that of a frightened little ragamuffin whose whole world is a very threatening place. That was it. All of the adult veneers had been stripped in the shadow of the evolving tragedy, and for a moment, at least, we were all frightened children.

As the fire raged, I became intrigued more by the faces and reactions of the displaced residents, than with the flames that engulfed the dwelling. I studied the stricken faces in the crowd and saw the raw emotions everyone wore so clearly. For once, I didn't feel like a misfit.

Though many of us were total strangers, we were all in the same boat. In a flash of insight, I saw how silly our perceived separateness was. No matter how special or different we think we are in relation to each other, we are only small parts of the bigger whole. Finally, I realized that "fitting in" was only an illusion, and it was almost amusing to see how miserable I'd made myself by trying to live up to standards that I thought were certain to make me one of the "normal" people. Now I understood that we all automatically fit in on the only scale that counts, the scale of humanity.

I watched as neighbors, firemen, and police risked their lives to make certain everyone got out safely. I saw people comforting one another and total strangers offering sweatshirts and jackets to each other. The Red Cross arrived and provided food, coffee, and the inside of a trailer to keep warm. There were lots of heartfelt hugs exchanged and shoulders for crying on, and it occurred to me that though many of these people didn't even know each other, they were offering exactly what parents offer children: love, comfort, food, shelter, and strength. At that raw and basic level, it was apparent that we were all each other's children in some meaningful way that had nothing to do with heredity, DNA, or fertility.

We were all family at that moment, and I experienced a lovely sense of belonging. The connection we were all sharing in those predawn hours wasn't ephemeral, I realized; only our awareness of that connection tended to be temporary, as we again became engrossed in our own individual lives. I had awakened to the bond, which we all share as human beings, that is eternal and real and can't be destroyed by fire or any other natural disaster. When all is said and done, that bond is all we have. And it is enough.

So that could be my legacy. My part in that bond was what I could leave behind to whoever inhabits the world after me. I could leave a legacy of love and of caring for others, which, from where I stood at that moment, was a lot more meaningful than any heirloom I could have rescued from flames. Whether I chose to give that loving influence to a child, an adult, a cause, or all three didn't matter. What mattered was that I would give myself back to the world in a loving and positive manner. I knew that it was all the seemingly small contributions we make that end up improving our world. We contribute through the way we drive our cars or work at our jobs or relate to everyone in our lives with honor and respect.

I began to see the foolishness of all those years of

thinking that I didn't fit in. I'd been seeing the world of humanity as if I were separate from it, as if I were on one side of a great divide and everyone else were on the other. It had taken forty-five years for me to realize that it is impossible to be alone in the world.

Somehow in my blind acceptance of all that I'd learned growing up, I had overlooked the significance of my own unique gifts in the overall scheme of things. Sadly, I'd thought I could not contribute anything to the future if I hadn't contributed a genetic look-alike. I was so obsessed with one purpose for being here that I had been completely oblivious to the abundance, the joy, and the deep connections to others that had been right under my nose.

It was time to focus on the ways in which my life was a perfect fit, rather than concentrating on all the measurements I had used in the past to exclude myself. At long last, I was ready to allow myself to be comfortable in the world.

After the fire officials allowed us back in the building, I changed clothes and immediately went for a leisurely stroll down by the docks. I was feeling very grateful not only to be alive, but also to suddenly have such clarity about the design of my life and the certainty that I was an important part of the big picture.

I began to walk along the harbor, sipping cappuccino and admiring the yachts that rocked gently in the peaceful, sapphire waters. Farther down on the docks, I noticed that there was a boat show in progress and that the public was invited to board and explore several of the yachts that were for sale. Normally, I would not have considered participating in such an event, since I would have felt like an impostor, knowing full well that I would never be able to afford such a luxury. But that was in the days when I told myself I didn't fit in. Today was different. I'd had a revelation, and I knew there was nowhere that I didn't fit in.

Feeling as calm and tranquil as the water itself, I removed my shoes and stepped up onto a floating bit of opulence. I walked through the cabin, taking in the meticulously designed decor and admiring the beauty of it. As I stepped to the stern of the boat, where its owner stood, I confidently engaged him in conversation.

As we stood looking out at the serenity of the water and chatting amiably, it occurred to me that, for the moment, ownership of this incredible vessel was only a matter of semantics. We were both standing in the sunshine on the stern of this beautiful boat, totally immersed in our elegant surroundings. What did it matter who had a piece of paper proving ownership? At that moment, we were both enjoying the boat immensely, and that was all that was important.

Afterward it dawned on me that I could employ this principle anytime I thought something was missing from my life. Nothing need ever be missing again.

Until this encounter, I hadn't understood the extent of the power of my mind. Now I saw that I could do the exact same thing with any situation, simply by appreciating it and claiming ownership of that moment. This applied to children as well. Suddenly all the children of the world, including those who were victims of abuse and neglect, were my family. I knew that on some basic level we are all one and other people's children are just a part of that oneness. I would never waste another tearful millisecond bemoaning the fact that no child had ever passed through my physical body.

There was a soft light glimmering at the end of the dark tunnel now, and no one could ever extinguish it again, not even me. The world was a beautiful place once more, filled with hope and promise, the way it had been during blissful childhood years when my best friend and I had played at our future roles. The only thing that had changed since then was my definition of that role—it had expanded.

Finally, I was allowing myself to fit in.

CHAPTER FIVE

Hacking a Path Through the Wilderness

By their mid forties, most people are beginning to slow the pace of their lives and to think about and plan for gliding into retirement. Not me. I was just beginning to realize how much there was that was available to me. I began leaving my old illusions and frustrations behind as I saw another realm unfolding before me. It offered a distinctly different way of life from the one I was accustomed to, stimulating my imagination and luring me to its welcoming borders. Though I was aware that I was not the first woman to explore these possibilities, it was uncharted territory for me, and I knew I had much to learn here. Everywhere I looked, there seemed to be lessons directing me toward a new level of contentment.

I began finding lessons in the most ordinary occurrences, things I had seen a thousand times before but had never taken the time to consider. Slowly I began to suspect the remedy for my past unhappiness had been available to me all along, if only I could have stopped focusing on myself and paid attention to the subtle guideposts that were pointing me outward.

I was living in New Jersey at this time, on a small peninsula between the ocean and a bay. In the early part of the summer that year, some of the residents noticed that three dolphins had some-how made their way into the bay and were play-fully and happily feeding there. No one was terribly concerned about the dolphins' eventually needing to get back to the ocean, when their instincts told them it was time to head south for the winter. There was plenty of time for that, and besides, the bay provided plenty of food for them during the summer. Everything would be fine just as long as they got out of there before winter arrived and everything froze.

The dolphins spent the whole summer in the

bay, playing, feeding, and delighting the residents with their unusual presence. As autumn approached and the dolphins had still not made their way back into the ocean, there was growing concern among all who watched that they needed to be guided out before the bay began to freeze.

Several attempts were made to guide the playful creatures back to the open sea, but all efforts failed. The problem was that the dolphins needed to swim north around the peninsula in order to get to the ocean, but their instincts told them to swim south.

The dolphins resisted every innovative human tactic to help them out of the bay. So there they stayed, unable to see the big picture and insisting on only swimming south, even though that caused them to remain hopelessly landlocked. Winter came, the bay froze, and much to the dismay of all who had tried to help, all three dolphins perished.

The lesson wasn't lost on me.

I'd been trying to follow a traditional path and had ended up banging my head against a brick wall. As I watched the dolphins resist swimming toward their freedom, I wondered if perhaps my behavior had been quite similar.

Now as I imagined myself with children of my own, I could admit that possibly I, too, would have felt hopelessly ensnared at times by the demands of raising a family. I had always sensed there were aspects of motherhood that would have left me feeling trapped and frustrated, and I hadn't been willing to take that step. As I watched the three dolphins struggling to find their way, I could see that I had been struggling like that for a long time too. After years of ambivalence, I acknowledged that I had been given a choice, and I had chosen freedom. Now I could make peace with that.

With that midlife realization, some of my pain spontaneously began to subside. Around that same time, I began training to run a marathon, and in the process, I ran headlong into another lesson.

In an effort to gain strength as well as aerobic fitness, I had begun a program of weight lifting in addition to my training runs. Since I wasn't entirely comfortable around weights, I worked with a personal trainer to teach me the proper form and to propel me to a new level of fitness.

I would always start our sessions feeling strong and confident, but after a few repetitions, the weights would become almost impossible to lift.

My arms would tremble and feel like wet noodles as I tried to hoist them into the air one more time. Without exception, that's when my trainer would insist that I do at least one more set.

"This is too hard," I would say. "I'm too old and too tired to do any more."

"Good," he would always answer. "These are the ones that count. These are the ones that are going to take you where you want to go."

And go there, I did. I got strong and fit and ran my first marathon without a whimper. Why did I have to go through the pain and struggle of those last few sets before getting to this new level of fitness? Because that's what it took.

What I learned was that if I really wanted to reach new heights in any area of my life, occasionally I would have to rise up one more time and go through some discomfort, often just when I was feeling most vulnerable and beaten down. But that persistence to prevail was the key.

Now the lessons were everywhere, and for once, I was willing to see them. Almost magically, I would feel myself being pulled in the direction I most needed to go, and doors to which I had once been oblivious began to open. As I opened myself to the way things were, instead of trying to force them into a mold that fit my expectations, an interesting thing happened. A vague longing tugged at the essence of my being, and it wasn't the longing to fit in or to have a child of my own anymore. It was stronger than that. Apparently this new spark of interest had been born of the pain and frustration I had had to endure before glimpsing an unexplored and peaceful place off in the distance.

In my twenties and thirties, I hadn't any idea where to look for answers or fillers for what I felt was a void in my life. I had assumed that void was the result of my childless state, rather than what I finally learned it was—my unwillingness to accept a life that contradicted everything I had grown up expecting. I had been looking in all the wrong places to fill that perceived emptiness—my career, my relationships, my possessions—and none of them had held the answer. It wasn't until I dragged myself into my mid forties, thinking I had lost all hope of a normal life, that a pinpoint of light flickered in my mind and gentle new urges surfaced.

The urges I was feeling were entirely different from the ones that had been tearing me apart for so long. Now I felt intensely curious about, rather than afraid of, what I might discover by walking along this different path. I was no longer willing to be consumed by thoughts of what I didn't have or what more traditional circles expected of me. There were plenty of other childless women in the world, and now I was sincerely interested in knowing them and learning from them.

Surely Christopher Columbus must have felt this same curiosity when he risked everything and set sail for the horizon, in spite of rumors that he would fall off the edge of what was perceived by most people to be a flat earth. Ben Franklin's curiosity had to have been stronger than his fears or his need for approval when he flew his kite in a lightning storm. And what about Neil Armstrong, the first man to walk on the moon? Certainly he must have felt some trepidation when he blasted off into space, then put his foot down in a place that had never supported life.

What inner promptings did these people hear? What deep-seated desires whispered to the American pioneers and inspired them to settle the West, to leave the relative comfort of their log cabins for a journey fraught with harsh weather, battles, and disease? What made them trust their gut instincts and risk everything? Did all of those people actually choose to accomplish what they did, or were some of them driven by circumstance? Either way, I found great comfort and inspiration in their accomplishments.

Whether they went voluntarily or not, I think they must have sensed that fate held a special place for them, and I was suddenly grateful to the childless women who had gone before me. Visionaries of the past may not always have had the approval of others, but what they had instead was a passion to triumph over the frontiers they were about to traverse.

The presence of other childless women in the world indicated a relatively new concept to me—that there is more to being a woman than bearing children. The idea that I could be a complete human being unto myself challenged my old thinking and helped me to shed the more traditional beliefs and attitudes that I had clung to for so long.

Whether our child-free circumstances occur by chance or by conscious choice, any stigma that we are somehow abnormal and incomplete is both painful and inaccurate. Those of us affected by that stigma have our work cut out for us as we blaze a trail through other people's assumptions and prejudices, as well as our own. Exploring a frontier is usually not easy work, but it is almost always guaranteed to build character and to be filled with surprises and opportunities.

Now I realized that I could see my child-free status either as an affliction or as a rare and unusual gift to be explored and cultivated. The choice was mine, and once I was willing to stop lamenting what I didn't have, I found the energy to look in new directions. I was anxious to begin probing and unveiling the unacknowledged facets of our feminine nature, revealing powers that women have historically often been too preoccupied with child rearing to notice.

One such power is the boundless love that women bear within them. I'm always fascinated when I see the reaction of a busy woman—an executive, for example, or someone involved in an important project—when she suddenly and unexpectedly catches a glimpse of her child.

The transformation is usually immediate and magnificent. A complete metamorphosis takes place right before one's eyes as that mother focuses her whole being on her child. That is the kind of feminine energy and power that I am certain can change the world into a more loving place.

I knew now that I wanted to direct my untapped passion and focus toward all the issues that are important to me. I thought about what could be accomplished if I used my energy to get politically involved in issues that concern me, to do volunteer work, or to contribute to the support of abandoned and neglected children.

It had finally dawned on me that it wasn't necessary for me to be a mother in order to express such enormous love and concern. Those feelings couldn't be something that is possible only if I'd given birth to a child who shared some of my heredity. How could it be? Love like that doesn't just appear out of nowhere. It has to have been lying dormant all along, waiting for me to give myself permission to release it. Could having a child be the only reason to do so? Could not having a child be any reason to withhold it?

From as far back as I can remember, motherhood was the most acceptable outlet for such selfless and beautiful emotions. As a result, any behavior that mimicked motherhood was encouraged, not only by family and teachers, but also by total strangers. Beginning with my first dolls, some of which actually cried "real tears" and wet their diapers, I was aware of the expectation to direct all of my emotions and energy toward motherhood.

With my new consciousness slowly emerging, I couldn't help but wonder whether the desire to become a mother is triggered by biology, society, or a combination of the two. I suspected it was the combination that had influenced my desires and choices, but I also had to admit that possibly a lack of imagination on my part had been what kept me stuck in ambivalence for so long.

Looking for evidence to support "nature" or "nurture," I deliberately became more aware of the behavior of little girls as I walked through parks and shopped in supermarkets. I noticed that every child I saw carrying a baby doll received positive feedback in the form of adult smiles. A clear message is sent whenever a child is holding a "baby" in her arms; people smile and approve of her. She somehow becomes more adorable and lovable herself because of the little "baby" she carries around with her.

Are we assuming that this child has a deep

and natural maternal instinct? Maybe she does and maybe she doesn't, but does she really even have a choice? Those approving smiles have, of course, been shaping the destinies of women throughout history. They have been teaching young girls what is expected of them as they grow older. Not that I think there is anything wrong with girls (or boys, for that matter) playing with dolls, or with adults smiling at them when they do, but I was beginning to understand the seeds of my own longing and confusion about my highest purpose in life.

I began to see the impact of the thousands of subtle messages that surround us all. Is it any wonder, I thought, that in this era of widespread sex education and almost foolproof birth-control methods we still see so many teenagers having babies? Pregnant teenagers are certainly not a new phenomenon, but they seem to have a new and alarming attitude about having babies.

Watch any talk show and sooner or later you are bound to see teenagers who are talking about *trying* to get pregnant. Of course, they're not the only ones. There are plenty of adult women who opt for motherhood, and some of them opt to do so simply because they don't know what else to do with their lives. Making one's way through the world is a frightening prospect for anyone, but all too often I have met women who see motherhood as an unrealistically solid life raft in an ocean of risk and uncertainty. Women have choices today that they've never had before, so in many cases there are at best only first-generation role models out there to guide them through the experience of carving out a role and making a living.

Somewhere along the line we women still seem to be getting a very clear message that motherhood will take that pressure off us and provide us with instant credibility, respect, and a very well-defined role in society. Not that there isn't plenty of obvious evidence of the substantial demands and responsibilities of motherhood, but at least our gender has long been familiar with them. It is the unknown that people often find most frightening.

The world can be a pretty threatening and perplexing place under the best of circumstances, and these are very confusing times for all of us. Traditional gender roles are being questioned and redefined, and new demands are being placed upon everyone. Men are learning more about child care, and women are learning more about the business world.

In a way, it may have been a little easier for young girls who grew up in the traditional households of the fifties and sixties. As we entered the workforce, my generation knew we were also going to war. We simply had no idea how hard and bloody the fight for change would be. We wondered why we even had to fight this battle, since it seemed obvious to us that everyone, both male and female, could only benefit from adding feminine talents and skills to the world outside the home, and we were anxious to prove it. Like baby-faced soldiers dressed in army fatigues, carrying weapons and several rounds of ammunition, we were more than ready to run headlong into battle for our rights, our choices, and our independence.

The war has been long and the casualties on both sides even higher than we ever imagined. All around us are the signs of continuing conflict in the form of lawsuits, resentment between the sexes, sexual harassment, and threatened egos. We are in our fourth decade of this fight for women's rights and still there is plenty of anger on both sides.

Like a fresh group of reinforcements, today's generation of females is arriving on the scene, and rather than being inspired to carry on our cause, they have reason to be discouraged by what they see. Somehow we seem to have been backed into a corner where we are still not fully appreciated in the workforce, yet we now have career responsibilities in addition to our traditional roles of homemaker and mother. One astute friend of mine who juggled a job as well as a family told me that if there is such a thing as reincarnation, she hoped she would never come back as a female lion. When I asked her why not, she said it was because in the animal kingdom, it is the female lion who hunts for the food, drags it home, and raises the cubs by herself, yet it is the male who is considered "king of the jungle."

"Been there, done that," she added.

It took great courage to hold our heads high and to develop the skills and identities that opened doors to the world outside the home. We have to continue to pave the way for present and future generations, and it seems to me that those of us who are free of the demands of motherhood are especially good candidates for the job.

As with the pioneers of the West, a hundred years from now, it won't really matter who was related to whom. What will matter is the legacy and the hope for future generations that we can leave behind.

CHAPTER SIX

Giving Birth to the Self

What had jolted me from my sleepwalk through life hadn't been anything like the blast of an alarm clock. No, it had been more like someone tickling my face with a feather, gently teasing me out of a deep and disturbed sleep.

For a long time, I'd paid no attention to the brief glimpses of a broader perspective that occasionally floated through my consciousness, beckoning for my attention. Instead, I brushed them aside, annoyed by the distraction. Meanwhile, I turned up the volume of what I thought was real life and continued to dwell in uncertainty and anguish.

I didn't know it during the turbulent and anxious years of my twenties and thirties, but if I had been able to shut out the messages my immediate world was sending me and stop crying and bemoaning my fate, I would have known that I was pregnant with new life all along. My own. In spite of the well-publicized progress made by feminists, it wasn't until the early signs of menopause in my mid forties that I realized I was finally ready to give birth to myself.

It takes about nine months to have a baby, but it takes much, much longer to finally give birth to a fully developed adult. There are three trimesters to pregnancy and each of them has very specific symptoms and a very specific purpose. They prepare the mother gradually, both mentally and physically, for a most demanding yet joyous time of her life. It is good that pregnancy is a process rather than an overnight event, since probably no one could instantly adjust to the dramatic changes that occur when a whole new life emerges into the world.

It was during my late thirties that the panic had set in, and I had wanted to mother a child more than ever before. Being a registered nurse, I saw myself as a "giver" by nature, and I assumed that made me a perfect candidate for the job of raising a child. I was aware that parenting is probably the most difficult job we ever face in our lives, but I was certain I could live up to the challenge.

Ever since the night I had found myself envying my patients, I had begun questioning the purpose of my life. I also wondered why I hadn't found myself in a healthy relationship, which I considered to be the only acceptable circumstance in which to have a child. I was unaware of the superb and perfect timing of the universe. So I assumed that what happened next was merely a coincidence. One day, feeling unhappy that motherhood had eluded me so far, I "randomly" turned on the TV and watched an episode of a popular talk show.

They were talking about the eating disorder known as anorexia nervosa. One of the guests, who was in the throes of the ailment, was telling the host and the audience that she desperately wanted someday to help others to overcome this devastating disease. Another guest, who had recovered from the disease herself, lovingly put her arm around the first woman and gently asked, "How do you think you can help others if you can't even help yourself yet? You can't give something that you don't have. Take the focus off others, and put it where it belongs right now. Focus on making yourself better.''

That comment suddenly struck home. Was it possible that I had been doing the same thing? For many years I had not done a very good job of mothering and nurturing the only person dependent on me, myself. I had always been more willing to take care of others than to take care of myself. It had always seemed infinitely easier to nurture, support, and explore the feelings of total strangers in my work as a nurse, than it was to give my own needs that same attention. Avoiding and ignoring my needs had been a way of not dealing with the major issues of my life. Now I had to ask questions like, Who was I, really? What hidden talents did I have? What was I capable of contributing to the world and how did I propose to create it? How could I know what truly gave me joy if I hadn't experienced any? And most important, How could I have thought I could care for others, particularly a baby, if I hadn't learned to care for myself yet?

I realized that I didn't know the answer to even one of those questions. It was a gentle revelation, but one that demanded my attention, and like a woman who calmly smiles to herself as she notices the first subtle signs of pregnancy, I was suddenly aware that a brand-new life was stirring within me.

And so, what I call my auto-pregnancy began. Ever since the night of the apartment building fire, when I'd had my first glimpse of the interconnectedness of people, and now with the realization that I had an obligation to develop my own life before trying to direct someone else's, my world had begun to expand. Since I was in my mid forties at the time, it was more like a change-of-life pregnancy, and in fact, it did just that. Awakening to a new direction and a world that is abundant with possibilities didn't happen in a matter of days, or even months, for that matter. It was a slow process, but I definitely sensed an energy in myself that had lain dormant for far too long.

I examined what I had recently been calling emptiness in my life and found a new appreciation for the undisturbed time I had for accomplishing anything I wanted. Though I had achieved my earlier goals of traveling, writing, and running a marathon, I now looked forward to pursuing more selfless interests. I went through a thirty-hour training program with the local police department and began doing volunteer work for them, and I got involved in several organizations dedicated to helping abused and abandoned children.

Since I recognized that this was a gestational period for me, a time for discovering a purpose and how my own unique talents could serve that purpose, I decided to treat it with the same reverence as the beginning of any new life, though I was certain that this process would take far longer than nine months. It had already taken more than forty years.

I gave a lot of thought to the similarities between women who are pregnant with babies and women who are pregnant with themselves.

The first trimester of most pregnancies is usually filled with excitement, hopes, and dreams, and my "first trimester" was no exception. I wanted more than anything to pass on a piece of myself to the world, a richness that was uniquely mine, something I could be proud of and that would be remembered long after I was gone. I no longer thought that necessarily had to be a child of my own. After all, there is no shortage of children on the planet, only a shortage of people to love them, it seems.

Obviously, the world is not in need of people to populate it, but there seems to be a real shortage of people to bring harmony, to show kindness and love, to ensure a better world for future generations. I was determined that my contributions, whatever they turned out to be, would have some importance.

These thoughts passed through my mind as I became more comfortable with the idea that reproducing is not necessarily the only path to joy for a woman. It is simply the only one so far that has been universally approved.

The second trimester of most pregnancies is characterized by a feeling of general well-being. The overwhelming fatigue has usually faded by this point, and during the middle to the end of this trimester, the mother feels the very first movements of the new life that is waiting to be born. I eventually reached that point too. Gone was the bone-weary exhaustion from living with the narrow views some people hold of women like me. Those opinions didn't matter anymore because I had chosen to fill myself with a new sense of purpose, with love and goodwill directed toward everyone and everything that inhabits our planet. It was so much better than being bitter. And bitterness had never made much sense anyway.

The second trimester is also the time when the mother realizes that now there is no turning back. The new life becomes physically apparent, and it is clear that, sooner or later, it is going to come out. Like most mothers-to-be, a sense of calm and serenity engulfed me. I finally knew, just knew, that everything was going to be all right.

I was beginning to take a more global view of my little world, and it was actually quite beautiful. I knew that throughout history there were women like me who hadn't taken part in the usual chain of events that child rearing brings. They had probably changed the world in other, just as profound ways. They might have been women who, like Joan of Arc, led armies, female pioneers who had the courage to settle the West, or everyday women like me who questioned traditional roles and made new paths for themselves.

The third trimester of pregnancy is hallmarked by fatigue, impatience, and a burning desire to get on with the task at hand. I, too, went through a period when my desire to leave my old attitudes behind and to get on with this new role was insistent. I read women's biographies, expanded my circle of friends, and took classes on topics that were unfamiliar to me, such as buying real estate, creating web sites, and doing stand-up comedy. I wanted to learn and to grow, and I had too much to do to let anything take priority over the birth of my true self.

Predictably, the labor pains occurred in the still of many nights. I lay tossing and turning, trying to get comfortable with the new identity I was sculpting for myself. Like any realistic mother, I knew I wasn't perfect, but I also knew I would give this new life in me the benefit of everything I had learned so far. My old attitudes and opinions died hard, but eventually I gave birth to a healthy and whole person who wanted more than anything to bestow her feminine talents and love upon the world. I vowed that I would do my best to remain open-minded and to use my time and talents in the most constructive ways possible. Sadness and regret over old expectations became a thing of the past, and as I accepted the circumstances of my life, a new feeling had begun creeping in, which I recognized as happiness.

Instantly, I forgot the pain that had brought this

new life to me. It didn't seem important any longer. What was important was that I was whole now. Whole and healed.

Shortly after my full awakening, I happened to be standing in a hotel lobby, looking into a mirror. As usual, I studied my reflection carefully, searching for the usual flaws. For once though, I saw no flaws. I recognized the person staring back at me as the one I had been searching for all of my life, the one I always thought I wanted to marry. There I was. My other half at long last!

I believe that when the feminine mother in us emerges, no matter what the process, she is full and whole and bountiful. She is not only filled with love, but she has love to spare, both for herself and for others.

It doesn't matter to whom we give our love, as long as we fill a need for someone, whether that person sprang from our own womb or someone else's. We can laugh at the belief that the only being worthy of receiving our love is a spouse or one who has our genes.

No doubt, there is a universal, radiant, and glowing mother within all of us, and its existence has little to do with biological birth. There is nothing to prevent any one of us from having that coveted "pregnant glow." We are—all of us—always pregnant with the potential to love every child, every adult, every form of life in the universe. The choice is ours, and it always has been.

So start the music and throw the confetti. It's time to celebrate!

PART THREE

The Celebration

CHAPTER SEVEN

Taking the High Road

The old cliché about life beginning at forty seems a little inaccurate to me. It has taken the better part of five decades for me to reach the level of peace and contentment I had been searching for, but the fact that I have reached it at all feels like a miracle. Flirting with fifty in the not-too-distant future, I finally see changes in myself and in my life that I like very much.

Other people's opinions have become far less important to me because I trust my own opinions now, and I am not shy about voicing them. Decisions are no longer an exercise in agonizing, but, rather, clear and simple choices. My relationships have improved, career opportunities have appeared out of nowhere, and peace of mind has become a reality. I marvel at how much easier every aspect of my life has become since finally making peace with the fact that things don't necessarily have to go according to my plan. Most important, I have learned to embrace change, rather than resist it, the way I did for most of my life, and that has made the biggest difference of all.

Looking back on earlier years, I remember when, not only the motherhood issue, but each and every decision I faced had been pure torture for me. One incident, in particular, reminds me how far I have come since those days.

I was living in Florida at the time, and I was involved with a man whom I loved desperately and who was incapable of making a commitment to me. Every ounce of intelligence within me knew that he would never be able to give me the kind of relationship I craved, and every ounce of sense told me to cut my losses, to leave him once and for all. So finally I did.

I packed all of my worldly possessions into my car and headed for Interstate 95, toward my hometown in New Jersey. To this day, I can still see the way he looked in my rearview mirror as I blinked back tears and tried to do the proverbial "right thing."

I stopped at every phone booth along the interstate and called him, crying and begging him to change his mind and make a commitment to me. The best he could offer was a heartfelt request for me to turn around and come back. We would "talk about it," he said. But I'd had enough of talking. I'd had a solid year of it, and every time the subject of marriage had come up, he'd backed off like the Cowardly Lion.

I knew nothing was ever going to change, so I resisted his attempts that day at a reconciliation. Nonetheless, I continued to stop at gas stations, restaurants, and roadside phone booths to call him. Sometimes I would beg him to reconsider the prospect of marriage, and other times he would beg me to, please, just come home and talk about it again. On every occasion, we both cried.

I made one last call to him from a phone booth in a roadside diner just outside of Jacksonville. I didn't have any more change left at that point, so I thrust a five-dollar bill at a waitress and asked her for change. She took one look at my puffy eyes and miserable expression and smiled sympathetically, handing me all the change in her nickel-and-dime-laden pockets, refusing to take the five-dollar bill I dangled before her. Apparently this kind soul had witnessed this type of scene before and knew all too well the pain I was suffering.

I dialed the number for at least the dozenth time that morning, and he answered without "Hello" this time, but with "Please come back," instead. He asked if I still had my key to his apartment, and I said yes. He told me that if I turned around now, I'd be "home" by ten o'clock tonight. He said he felt certain that I would make the right decision and give our relationship another chance, and that he was going to have a steak dinner and a dozen roses waiting for me, because he knew I would come to my senses and return.

I hung up the phone more confused than ever, and I honestly didn't know what to do. I hesitated for a moment as I saw the sympathy in the eyes of the waitress again. I desperately wanted to talk to her because I sensed she was someone who would understand, but I didn't dare. Instead, I pushed open the diner door and headed for my car. This was a decision I'd have to make on my own.

Through my tears, I steered the car onto the

access road that led back to the interstate, and I saw a familiar sign looming up ahead. It was one of those red, white, and blue interstate highway signs with two arrows pointing in opposite directions. One arrow pointed south, toward my boyfriend and everything that I had left behind. The other arrow pointed north, away from the security of that relationship and into the unknown territory of a life that I would have to discover on my own.

As I drove closer and closer to that sign, I became more and more confused, then more and more panic-stricken. I had to make a decision, and I had to make it now.

But I couldn't.

I ran over the sign, flattening it against the tall tropical grass that surrounded it, and it made a terrible protesting noise against the underside of my car. I didn't care. I leaned my head against the steering wheel and cried for a long time.

Eventually, I got quiet, pulled myself together, and made a decision. I headed north toward the unknown, hoping I would be able to handle whatever came up.

Looking back on that experience now, I realize how far I have come. Making decisions today is no longer the overwhelming task it once was. It has become infinitely easier because I am willing to embrace the changes that accompany my choices. I have also learned that my best decisions are made when I learn to sit still and be quiet.

That moment of quiet after I ran over the sign was the first one I had ever consciously allowed myself to experience, and it helped me to make exactly the right decision, though I didn't know it was the right decision at the time. I also didn't know the source of that wisdom that had pointed me in the right direction, but I do now.

It was that gentle, intuitive voice that resides in all of us, and, for me, getting quiet is the key to hearing it.

Why is it so important to get quiet? Because when you are immersed in confusion and commotion, it is hard to hear anything besides the panic-stricken pounding of your heart. Outer noises can drown out even the most persistent inner wisdom.

That lesson was made very clear to me after I had been driving one day on a busy freeway with my car windows rolled down and the radio blaring. Traffic was so heavy that I could barely hear the radio, so I turned the volume up as high as it would go, but still, I couldn't hear it well enough to suit me. In frustration, I turned the radio off without adjusting the volume and pulled into my garage. The next time I got into my car and turned the radio on, the sudden pandemonium practically blasted me out of my seat. How could I have not been able to hear that? I wondered. It was hard to believe, but at the time, of course, there had been so much noisy high-speed traffic going past me.

That is when I realized the importance of getting quiet in order to hear my calm inner voice of intuition. If I am surrounded by chaos and drama, as I often was in younger years, it is that much harder to see my choices clearly or to take calm and deliberate action. Now that I have learned to turn down the noise in my life, I no longer have to agonize over decisions, consult total strangers for their opinions, or run over any more road signs. The high road is very clearly marked.

By getting quiet and trusting my instincts, I inadvertently developed several other skills that have improved the quality of my life. I learned to get honest, both with others and with myself. I began to speak my mind in relationships rather than worrying about what the other person would think of me, and, naturally, my relationships improved. I taught myself to say "no" to people and behaviors that no longer served me, and watched as much of my resentment dropped away. I wasn't afraid to state my needs anymore, and, as long as I was being honest with myself, I had to admit that there were two major areas in my life that needed fixing, my career and my environment.

After more than twenty years in the nursing profession, I decided that I no longer wanted to work in health care. Nor did I want to endure any more east coast winters. I was tired of being unhappy, and, for once, I was willing to do something about it.

I resigned from my nursing job, packed my belongings, and pointed my car west, with no particular destination in mind. As I drove across the country, little by little, I began to see glimmers of hope for true happiness in my life. The drive gave me time to think about all of the choices and opportunities (including my childless status) that had been there all along, and to realize that now I was willing to take responsibility for them. I was no longer willing to rely on a particular role to tell me who I was. I was willing to find out for myself.

All I'd had to do was gather up my courage and embrace whatever changes occurred in the process of truly becoming myself.

The first thing I bought when I settled in California was a deadbolt, and it wasn't for the door. I put it on my desk to remind myself that the door to the past is locked, and that I never have to go back to being unhappy.

I lived off my savings for a while as I indulged my passion for writing. It was then that I also took a thirty-hour training course with the local police department and began doing volunteer work with them. I vowed to do only the things I loved and the things that were meaningful to me. Though my money had dwindled to practically nothing, I was happier and more at peace with myself than ever before.

There are no rituals or ceremonies for marking the beginning of a new way of looking at life, but there ought to be. The inner changes that take place when we learn to accept life on its own terms are subtle and gentle transformations at best, but they are no less joyous or significant than any other milestone such as marriage and childbirth.

It was sad to think there had been a time when I thought I'd never celebrate anything, much less the decision to explore a different path. I had always thought I wanted to travel the same predictable road that everyone else had taken, complete with directions and familiar surroundings. But now the possibilities of what lay ahead in this less traveled direction were something to celebrate and to honor in some way.

The kind of celebration I experienced wasn't filled with boisterous or dramatic behavior, and it didn't take place anywhere outside of myself. But make no mistake, there was a party going on. Though no one else could hear the music, that didn't matter in the least. I heard a symphony. This celebration was far more subtle than anything I'd ever experienced before, but it was no less happy. It was the kind of happiness that sneaks up on you, making you smile to yourself, rather than exploding in a big burst of frenetic activity. It felt more like a cool ocean breeze during a summer heat wave, wafting past my overheated mind and drying the beads of perspiration that were born of too many years of trying to force life to take the shape I thought it should have.

As I stood back, I noticed something else that was amazing to me. I was pleasantly surprised to find that the illumination of one part of my mind had cast a soft glow on several other unresolved issues of my life as well. It was as if I'd walked into a darkened room, desperately searching for a particular object, and not been able to locate it. By flicking on the light, not only had the one item I'd been searching for been suddenly revealed, but everything else in the room was lit up too.

I saw myself beginning to take the high road in some of the other previously frustrating areas of my life, and I was overwhelmed at the thought of how much control I must have had all along over the amount of happiness that flowed through my existence.

For one thing, my attitude toward my romantic relationships began to be much healthier than it had ever been before. For years I had been struggling to understand why these relationships always seemed to cause me such pain. Now suddenly, I saw the problems quite clearly. Like an expert mechanic who can take one look under the hood of your car and tell you exactly what is wrong, I was able to diagnose the problems with my relationships.

I had been looking to those relationships to help me avoid the task of carving out an identity for myself in a world where I was not a part of the maternal majority. I had also not been a good communicator and had substituted unspoken expectations for honest conversation.

Self-esteem had been another area of lifelong struggle for me, and that, too, began to improve. After a few of my articles were published in various magazines, my passion for writing had been validated. I'm certain that all of the writing I had been doing at the time helped keep me in touch with my feelings and provided an outlet for creative expression.

Career frustrations in nursing had been put to rest the day I vowed never to work at a job I no longer loved, but the icing on the cake came with the publication of my first novel. Finally, my passion was supporting me.

Everything was so much easier now. Why hadn't I discovered this magical path years ago? I suspect the answer was inertia. I'd been too caught up in my misery and pain to even notice the bountiful choices that were available to me. It wasn't until anguish over all the unfulfilled desires of my life had brought me to my knees that I was able to honor this different path that I was traveling. Ironically, what I found was a joy far deeper than any I had ever hoped for.

At first I worried that my "different path" was merely a consolation prize for having missed *the* gold ring of life, giving birth. Now I know that what I had was a very rare gift, one that not every woman is willing or able to receive. I intend to use this gift to benefit children, who in turn will one day be adults. I feel it is people like me who have a special opportunity to open a way for them, to shine a beam of light that will make it easier for them to discover their own unique path in life.

Becoming a mother is only one of many possible gifts waiting for us. There are so many paths, in addition to having children, that lead to fulfillment, but many women are unable to start the process of developing the rest of their talents until after their children are grown. I am lucky. I have had the time and opportunity to explore the other gifts that have been waiting for me, and I'm seeing the fruition of that process now. Though I haven't experienced firsthand the joy of motherhood, I have come to terms with the realization that everything, in all our lives, involves a trade-off.

Is it really possible to have absolutely everything in life? And if it were, would I want it all? Or even have time for it all? Does a great musician moan about the fact that he never played pro football? Does an Olympic athlete cry because she never experienced being an accountant? Not if they have passion for what they are doing, they don't. Is there anything but our preconceived notions to prevent us from having great passion in our lives?

While I wisely chose not to have children in the kind of relationships I was drawn to during the bulk of my reproductive years, I had the gift of time to develop myself professionally, personally, and spiritually. An enormous amount of energy was available to me for forming an identity that would serve me well for the rest of my life. Admittedly, I didn't always see that time as precious, but I certainly do now, because that was what made this whole journey possible.

I know now that, along with all the mothers of the world, I am a glorious creature and that part of my purpose includes an appreciation of all children and a vision for their future. In some ways, I am no less responsible for their welfare than are their natural parents. My job, though, is a more expansive one.

While the pregnant mothers of the world are getting the nurseries ready for their new babies, I have an obligation to clear a path, create a future, and help get the world ready for them as well.

I can do that now because I am whole. I am healed. And I am happy.

CHAPTER EIGHT

Mothers of the Universe

In spite of my ambivalence, I have always known on some level that motherhood was part of my ultimate purpose in life, but it took me a long time and a lot of soul-searching to understand that mine would not be the usual kind of motherhood. It is the kind that encompasses more children than I could ever bear physically. And like any good mother, I am able to love all of my children equally and unconditionally.

I use the term "my children" in the same way any biological mother uses it, because we all know that no one ever owns a child, and in that sense, we all play a role in their welfare. The way I see it, as long as there is one child on this planet, we are all parents in some regard.

There are ways of being a mother that people don't often talk about or acknowledge, yet those of us who are aware in this regard are ready to make our unique contributions to shape the lives of children. There are no special days set aside on the calendar for us, but we know who we are.

We are the confidantes and the nonjudgmental, wiser friends of children. We are their relatives or their mother's best friend or someone who is simply around a lot in their young lives. They talk to us. And we listen to them. They have nothing to lose by revealing their innermost feelings to us. They have no reason to resent or argue with us. There is little or nothing they feel they have to hide from us. They trust us, and they know without a doubt that they have nothing to fear, because we have no need (and often no right) to be involved in disciplining them or in any number of other parental responsibilities.

During my younger, painful years, when I was aching to have a child of my own, I worked for a time as a registered nurse on a unit for terminally ill teenagers. Though it may sound like a morbid job, it turned out to be one of the most positive and satisfying experiences of my long career.

I still remember every one of those children's faces and names, but there was one in particular who really got to me. His name was Luke, and he was fifteen and dying from a malignant bone tumor. He knew his diagnosis and that his life expectancy wasn't more than a few months at best, yet he never mentioned anything about it. Instead, on days when he felt well enough, he would tease and laugh and strum on the guitar that always sat on the foot of his bed.

Luke had lots of support from friends and family, and during evening visiting hours, his room was more like an obstacle course than a hospital room. I had to maneuver myself and my equipment through the crowd of visitors every time I tried to check his intravenous line or take his temperature. The mood was always surprisingly jovial and upbeat as everyone chattered and deliberately stayed away from the subject of Luke's illness.

I remember one evening when Luke had been in a rare gloomy mood and only his mother and his aunt had come to visit. I was about to enter the room with his medication, but I stopped and listened for a moment when I heard the somber tones of a serious conversation between Luke and his mother.

"Don't talk about summer vacation," I heard him say. "You and I both know I'm not going to live that long."

"Stop that kind of talk!" his mother shot back, out of her own desperation, I am certain. "You're not going to die! You're going to be fine. You just wait and see."

I tapped on the doorframe and entered then, just as Luke shook his head in frustration and disgust.

I didn't say anything, but I made a mental note to go back and talk to Luke later on in the shift, after his mother and aunt had left.

By the time I found a few free moments to spend with him, Luke was just getting ready to go to sleep. I sat down on the side of his bed, and in the softest, gentlest voice I could find, I told him that I had overheard his earlier conversation with his mother. I asked him if he was okay and if there was anything on his mind that he wanted to talk about.

"They don't understand," he said. "I'm dying, and no one in my family will let me talk about it."

That was my cue. I sat there for a long time that

night, far past the end of my shift, and listened as Luke poured out his fears, his hopes, and his questions. I knew there wasn't anything more I could do than just be there for him and listen. He didn't want the false assurances his family offered or the technical answers the doctors were always supplying. He just wanted someone to listen to him and to appreciate what he was feeling. That kind of exchange was just too heartbreaking for many mothers to endure.

But I could do that for Luke and for his mother. And so I did. Luke talked and opened up to me that night in a way that he never had before, strictly because I wasn't his mother. And I was able to comfort him and listen to his anguish until he'd gotten it all out.

Many years later, when I looked back on that experience, I realized it had been one of many opportunities I'd had to nurture and support and love a child in a way that might not have been possible if I'd been the mother. At moments like that, it didn't matter that no one was going to call me "Mom." I had given something to a child that he desperately needed, and he had given something back to me that I, too, had desperately needed.

If I had been a mother myself at that time, I doubt that I could have worked on that particular unit, because the very thought of children being so ill would have hit too close to home. Also if I'd had family concerns of my own back then, there is a good possibility that at least some of my attention and focus would have been elsewhere at that moment. Perhaps there would have been children of my own to get home to and lunches to prepare for the next day. But instead, I had no other pressing responsibilities, and I was able to give Luke my total attention and my unlimited time. It was a gift for both of us.

That special time with Luke was only one of many treasured moments I'd experienced through a lifetime of not having children of my own. It was the very fact that I was childless that had allowed me to contribute to dozens of children in a rare and special way. Though that evening with Luke was one of the more dramatic moments of my "un-motherhood," there were many, many more that were less obvious but no less important.

In fact, that same night I had another unique moment of motherhood when I stopped at an all-night grocery store on my way home from work.

It was the night before Mother's Day, never an

easy time for me. The reminders were everywhere, especially in the produce aisle of this supermarket, which was strewn with bouquets of flowers, mostly pink and white ones, surrounded by color-coordinated balloons that read, "Number 1 Mom." There were also the usual plastic tags attached to the delicate carnations reading, "Happy Mother's Day."

There was something about those pink and white flowers of Mother's Day that had always had the potential to hurt. After all, I was nobody's mother so far, and probably never would be. I saw holidays of any kind as something to be avoided, lest I fall into a valley of depression over all that I thought was missing in my life. Now I would see that my teenage patient Luke had just helped me to broaden my definition of motherhood.

I had only dashed in to grab a quart of milk for my cereal in the morning, but all too predictably, I had been drawn to the colorful display of Mother's Day flowers that adorned the front of the store, and suddenly I wanted flowers to lift my spirits a bit after such a heartbreaking evening with Luke. Once again, market researchers made an "impulse buyer" out of me, and I decided to indulge myself.

I could always remove that tacky "Happy Mother's Day" tag.

Since it was late at night, most of the bouquets were a bit wilted, and I wondered if perhaps I should wait until the next morning, when surely there would be a fresher-looking batch. I was just about to exercise some restraint and turn my back on them when I spotted the one fresh bunch in the whole display. I reached for it, and just as I had the cellophaned stems within my grasp, a grubby little brown fist appeared out of nowhere and snatched them from my hold.

Too surprised to utter a word, I looked down at the beautiful, round face that stared up at me. His expression was a study in childlike sweetness, and two symmetrical dimples played at the corners of his hesitant smile. He held two fingers of his free hand in his upturned mouth and shyly asked, "Are these good ones? Will my mommy like these ones?"

I took a moment to recover, then smiled and answered directly from my heart, "Oh, you have wonderful taste in flowers! Your mommy's going to love them!"

With that, his face lit up with visible pride, and

he took off running toward his father and the cashier—with my flowers.

The funny thing is, I suddenly felt wonderful. In that five seconds of time, I had given a little boy what every child deserves. I had given him adult approval, encouragement, and confidence in his choices. Like any "real mother," I had just naturally put this child's welfare before my own, and I wouldn't have had it any other way. True, I did not have what I came to call custodial care of this child; I would not be giving him his bath tonight or teaching him to say his prayers or sending him to college one day, but for those few moments, at least, I was a mother in the most honest and beautiful sense of the word.

As I stood in the checkout line, I had time to ponder the events of the evening, and a pattern began to emerge. The beautiful maternal feelings that I had allowed myself to feel that night and to express to two precious boys who hungrily accepted my offerings was a wonderful gift to all of us. I suddenly saw with clarity that I'd had a choice, but that I had naturally chosen to enrich their lives in any way that I could. This awareness filled me with a sense of purpose and well-being. I had played a positive role in their young lives, and there was no telling when the next opportunity to nurture a child would occur. It could be a mere two minutes from now, if I could just remember to stay aware that we are all parents in some sense to every child who crosses our path.

With that in mind, I put the wilted flowers I'd bought in my favorite vase when I got home and never even considered removing the "Happy Mother's Day" tag from them. It was an appropriate way to celebrate the satisfaction and joy I'd felt at my own way of being a mother. I thought for a long time that night about the love and support I had shared with Luke and others like him, and the way the smile on the little boy in the grocery store had warmed my heart. Obviously, it wasn't only my role as a nurse that allowed me to make a meaningful contribution to a child's life. The opportunities were everywhere, and I realized that there are a million ways in which all of us can have a positive and possibly profound impact on any number of children.

We are the unsung mothers of the world. We are the teachers who take the time to show children how wonderful and special they are. We are the nurses who nurture them and tend to them, the grocery store clerks who patiently teach them to make change, the police officers who protect them and make them feel safe in a dangerous world. We are the waitresses who indulge them and make them feel important, no matter how tired our feet are.

We are the activists who fight for children's rights, the strangers who help them cross the street safely, and the social workers who love them and help them to find their way in a frightening and unfair world. We are the career-oriented professionals who stop and let them pet our dogs, the athletic coaches who give them an enticing glimpse of their own potential, and the kindly adults who take their hand when they are lost in a shopping mall and help them find their mommy again.

We are the ballet teachers who make them feel free and beautiful, and we are the roller-skating adults who pick them up when they fall off their bicycle and comfort them until their frantic parents arrive. We are the trusted friends in whom they can confide simply because they know we have no reason to judge them.

We are the people who help a young mother as she struggles to push her baby's stroller through a department store door, and we are the busy executives who jingle our car keys and smile at the cranky little urchin perched upon his mother's shoulder in front of us in the checkout line at the supermarket. We are the ones this mother may never even notice as we silently entertain her baby behind her and possibly witness his first smile. But we are not terribly concerned with any particular baby's first smile, first step, or first word, because we know that every smile, every step, and every word in any baby's life is important, and we treat them all with equal reverence.

We are the role models and idealists who support and believe in children's dreams because we support and believe in our own dreams. We are the creators of hope and love for them, and we give birth to the potential of all children.

Some of our contributions go unnoticed, but that doesn't matter. The world often overlooks worthwhile accomplishments. Great artists, poets, musicians, architects, and yes, even mothers, were often long gone before they were appreciated. That is nothing new. Besides, Nature is a mother too, and she most certainly loves us. Otherwise she would not have bestowed on us such a deep-seated desire to love a child, whether or not she blesses us with one of our own.

My very best friend was divorced shortly after giving birth to her daughter, and she raised her child virtually alone. We had been best buddies since we were seven years old, and we had gone through many life changes together. We spent a lot of time together when her daughter was growing up, and I have always been a part of their lives. My friend sometimes tells me all the things her daughter (who is grown now) does that remind her of me. She says she thinks that someday someone will discover that children not only inherit the traits of their biological parents, but also the genes of the people with whom they spend the most time. I wonder if this process has something to do with the way women who live together tend to have synchronized menstrual cycles.

Who knows? My friend is a very smart person, and she has always been ahead of her time. I'd put my money on her in a minute.

Now I know that women are capable of giving birth to more than babies. We give birth to beauty, love, patience, and creativity. Those of us who never actually give birth have so many other gifts to bestow upon the world. When we open our hearts to children, we begin to transform the world, and that is important.

Letting our love shine through, no matter what, will help take the world to a place where there is no such thing as an orphan or a motherless child or even a childless mother. Because we will all be one—nurturing, helping, teaching, and loving one another.

We will come closer and closer to achieving a more loving and generous world. And not another useless teardrop will fall, because we will have learned the true meaning of motherhood . . . and at long last, we will be living it.

CHAPTER NINE

The Marvels of the Multifaceted Woman

Like a diamond in the rough, a woman who has not given birth is a powerhouse of potential.

Whether or not they ever mother a child, little girls come into the world equipped in a unique and efficient way. There is no doubt that females are especially well designed for endurance. Our bodies require less food and less oxygen than men's, thus ensuring that our needs for physical survival are minimal. We have that extra layer of fat that modern society has taught us to reject, but which is really there for warmth, buoyancy, and vigor. We are also amazingly adept at tolerating pain, and anyone who has ever watched the birth of a baby cannot possibly walk away without new reverence for the strength and stamina the female body possesses.

And that is only the physical part.

We also tend to be rich in patience, intuition, kindness, creativity, resourcefulness, intelligence, and compassion.

With capabilities like that, how sad it is that we have historically been conditioned to believe we have only one significant purpose in life—to pro-create. Society has tended to treat us like a collective idiot savant, a generally feebleminded person who is a genius in one area, like playing the piano, painting, or solving complicated mathematical problems in one's head. In the case of women, bearing children was the one rare and awesome ability we were thought to possess. All of our other talents and capabilities were often overlooked or seemed to pale in comparison to our reproductive powers.

In my career as a registered nurse (an over-whelmingly female dominated profession), I have always had great respect for the sixth sense that women seem to have when it comes to caring for the sick. Almost always a nurse can accurately pick up the subtle changes in a patient's condition that do not register yet on any laboratory report or X ray. Of course, often when she reports her observations and suspicions to a member of the male-dominated profession of medicine, she is likely to be disregarded and called "nursie" or "unscientific" if she cannot provide tangible data to prove her opinion. Almost always the patient eventually proves her right, and then her astute observation is labeled nothing more than a lucky guess.

But it's not a lucky guess. It's a product of the many innate facets of the female being that are so often minimized or, worse yet, ignored. And caring for the sick is not the only place we see this happen. How often have we seen women manage a household with the financial genius of a stockbroker only to be called a housewife? How many times have we witnessed a woman handle a volatile, emotional situation with the finesse of a trained arbitrator and then be called docile or passive? And we've all seen the women who successfully juggle the demands of family, finances, and career with the grace of a figure skater and still are mainly known as a Mom. And then, of course, there are the women who often decide out of maturity, responsibility, and generosity not to have children of their own. And they are often called lots of unflattering things.

The good news (and there is lots of it) is that the world has definitely been changing in a positive direction. In some places there are still only faint hints of it, and in other places solid, tangible milestones have been achieved.

Watch television commercials closely and chances are you will often see at least one person in a wheelchair. A recent Miss America, Heather Whitestone, who is deaf, was the first person with a physical disability to win the Miss America title. Our society is more careful than in any other time in history to be "politically correct" and not to deliberately offend. At long last, even animals have certain rights, and there are lots of people who support and guard those rights. World leaders are apologizing for some of the devastation wrought by previous wars, and the Berlin Wall is now nothing more than a bad memory.

Most heartening, women are stretching their wings wider and more powerfully than ever before. That is partially due to the fact that more and more of us are at long last finding our own path.

No longer do the majority of us blindly accept the tasks we have historically been expected to perform without question.

Notice who is playing what roles in television commercials, where you are sure to see a shift in the stalwart attitudes and perceptions of the last decade or two. Now we take it for granted that our doctors, dentists, pilots, or financial consultants may very well be women, and the best part is that the ads are no longer simply paying lip service.

Even more impressive than that I think is the fact that it is finally acceptable for men to play an active and equal role in raising their children. It never fails to warm my heart when I see fathers pushing baby strollers and showing up in delivery rooms and lovingly cooking meals for their children. How can that not have a positive impact on both the fathers and their children?

Sexual harassment on the job was once unmentionable, and any woman who experienced it (which was the majority of us) was usually better off just enduring it or handling it by herself rather than reporting it, since all too often she would be targeted as the responsible party. Oh, how that has changed! And not a minute too soon. Not that it doesn't still occur, but our awareness of it as a society has certainly been raised, and there are established and effective avenues for us to pursue today in order to correct it.

When I look back to 1968, when I was one of the first women in my town to qualify as a lifeguard, it was quite a different world. I remember other women telling me that I should just "look good in a bikini and date the lifeguards, not become one," and I also remember how one of the neighboring towns would not allow me to compete in a lifeguard tournament simply because I was a female. The saddest part of that story perhaps is that I accepted that explanation, even though everyone (including me) knew that I could easily have placed in several of the events. How sad that I accepted the world as such a divided place and that I walked away without a fight!

It still astounds me that there was ever a time in this country when women were not allowed to vote or, if they were married, to own property (and of course, there are still many places in the world where this is still so). I've often heard men grumble that there was a time when men "respected women so much that they tipped their hats to them." My response to that comes directly from my heart. If I had to make a choice, I'd rather have the right to own property and to vote than have a man tip his hat to me.

What does all of this have to do with women who don't have children? Simple. These positive changes in society are an important part of the big picture. If taking the high road has taught me anything, it has taught me that the facets of our lives do not function independently of one another. Every time we grow beyond one struggle in our lives, that growth has a ripple effect on all of our other unresolved issues as well. It is only because women have evolved enough to insist on these basic changes, that we now have the choice to live our lives in any way we like.

One of the things most of us would like is to be treated with respect for who we are and what we do, whether we have children or not. Hopefully, we are witnessing just the beginning of a major shift toward an honest and fair society. Perhaps it is a step toward a time when all choices are made with the common good in mind, rather than on the basis of fear and ignorance.

In spite of what the eleven o'clock news might lead us to believe, I think the world is a more compassionate place than it has ever been before. And I don't think it is a coincidence that many of the positive changes have occurred as women have increasingly made their presence felt in the larger world, developing their talents, and putting their enormous, loving energy out into the universe, where it belongs.

No wonder the world has such problems! Up until now, we've only functioned on fifty percent of our resources. Imagine the possibilities when the healing, loving, maternal, and compassionate energy of women is fully released from the confines of limited expectations!

What an incredible and eye-opening journey my life so far has been! How foolish and tragically uninformed I was to have carried on so about life "passing me by." I am now awed by the magnificence of what lies before me, and I am humbled by the marvelous gift of femininity that has been bestowed upon me. None of the revelations or the enchantment would have occurred if I hadn't been given the challenge of being a woman who never gave birth to a child.

I might not have had to think that decision through or to develop any of the myriad talents that were lying just below the surface of all those old expectations. I might not have learned to give birth to myself or to develop my own potential, which no one, not even me, really knew existed. I might not have been able to step back and feel the compassion that I do for all the children of the world, because knowing myself as I do, surely I would have been far too caught up in my own children to notice any of the others.

There is still much about the design of my life that I don't understand, but there is one thing I know for certain. What I once saw as a loss and an empty hole in my heart has evolved into a bottomless well of caring for all children.

When I watch the news or merely look around me with my eyes wide open, I see an ocean of children, both young and grown, who are begging to be loved, guided, and protected. How could I have possibly thought that I did not have anywhere to put my heart, my love, and my talents? Any children in need of help are my children. Our children. And like any good parent, I will do anything to help, to support, to make it stop hurting, whether that means donating my money, my time, or simply my prayers.

This isn't a case of my filling a void with "other people's children." You see, there is no void anymore. I'm not sure when that happened, but I suspect it was around the time that I took the high road and realized that I had talents within me that I needed to get busy developing so I could help feed this very hungry world.

I can use the time and freedom that I have to take risks and to search out possibilities that I would never have been able to explore had I been responsible for a child. I can be bold, adventurous, and passionate, whether or not others find me or what I have to offer acceptable.

These views were recently validated for me when some of my nieces and nephews mentioned that they want to grow up to be like me!

Imagine that.

They think that I have an interesting life. And I do. I'm just surprised that they see it that way, especially when I compare their view to the way I used to see my aunt Agnes's life. They see the way I live as free and exciting. They like that I travel and write books and that I can still beat every one of them at the headstand contests we often have when we get together. They think that is very "cool."

When I think back to my own childhood and the way I dreaded becoming a "spinster" like my aunt Agnes, I am able to laugh at that fear for the very first time in my life. I have come full circle now, and it is a healing and wonderful feeling. The world is definitely changing in a positive direction if single, childless women like me are finally in a position where young children admire them, consider them "cool," and want to emulate them, rather than fear that their own lives might take the same direction.

Children are usually the first to point out the obvious, so I don't think it will be long before the rest of the world catches on to their astute observations.

And that brings me back to the subject of baby showers. Hard though it may be to believe, I feel a whole new sense of joy these days when I hear that someone I care about is pregnant. I can share their joy now because I am pregnant too.

Every day I give birth to all the hope, love, and potential that is within me. I realized long ago that every child is precious and important and that someone has to run ahead of them in the world to make the way safe. You can call those people parents or you can call them people who care. Either way, I am one of those people, and I am honored to perform such a desperately needed service. A new baby, no matter whose, is another little light in the world, and it will always be something for me to celebrate, and that fills my heart with rapture.

Now when I walk into a baby shower, I feel more like a reigning Miss America than a perennial runner-up.

Have you ever noticed the transformation that takes place during that first year of a Miss America's celebrity? The night she is crowned, usually she is awkward, very emotional, and a little unrefined. One year later when she returns to pass the crown on to her successor, she is almost unrecognizable. After one short year of experiencing the world in a whole new way, she has become polished, mature, sophisticated, and self-assured.

Well, that is me these days at a baby shower.

I have now experienced the world from a whole new perspective, and I like what it has done for me. My smile is genuine, and my happiness almost uncontainable. I can hold someone else's baby now and not feel that old, familiar pain anymore.

Instead I can drink in the sweetness of that child's softness, smell, innocence, and human potential. Now I know that every time a new life comes into the world, brand-new possibilities are born. And every time brand-new possibilities are born, the world will need people like me to clear the way and to help make it easier for each new life to follow his or her own unique little heart wherever it may lead.

There are so many moments now when I am exquisitely aware of my purpose and of the joy in my life. Moments that I could never have imagined would be so perfect or so right. They say that pain is difficult to remember, and I believe this is true. I have lost the memory of my earlier pain in much the same way a new mother forgets the agony of childbirth the instant she looks into the eyes of the new life she has delivered.

Emptiness and grief have been known to leave very quietly, and often they are gone long before we even hear the closing of the door. That is when peace and contentment can waft through the open window of our hearts like a summer breeze, filling us with softness, warmth, and joy. That is what has finally happened in my life.

And I hope in yours.